GREAT BIBLE STORIES

NOAH AND THE ARK

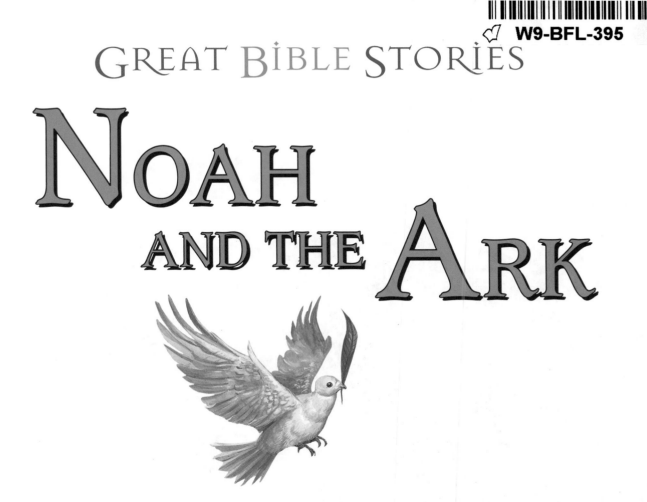

Adapted by Maxine Nodel   **Illustrated by Norman Nodel**

BARONET BOOKS is a registered trademark of Playmore Inc., Publishers
and Waldman Publishing Corp., New York, N.Y.

Copyright © MCMXCIII Playmore Inc., Publishers
and Waldman Publishing Corp., New York, New York

BARONET BOOKS, NEW YORK, NEW YORK
Printed in China

After Adam and Eve were banished from Eden, mankind began to multiply all around the earth. But man grew more and more evil and his wickedness angered God.

God began to regret making this beautiful world, and he was very sorry that he had made man.

Then God decided it was time to destroy mankind and end the wickedness that man brought forth.

But there was one man who pleased God, whose thoughts and deeds were good. His name was Noah.

God told Noah, "The evil on earth cannot continue. A great flood will come and destroy all living things."

God told Noah to build an ark made of good timber. When the flood would come, Noah, his wife and three sons would be safe.

So Noah told his sons, Shem, Ham and Japheth that they would help build the ark. And when the ark was done, God spoke to Noah again.

"Take two of every kind of living creature— animals, birds, and all creeping things— male and female, and bring them with you onto the ark."

The Lord God told Noah to bring food for forty days and forty nights. God had decided to make a great rain-storm that would flood all the earth.

So Noah gathered two of every animal he could find until they were all safe together in the ark.

Noah led his wife and sons into the ark and closed the doors behind them.

The people outside laughed at Noah and his ark,
but Noah trusted God and waited for the promised flood.

Seven days later it began to rain. It rained for forty days and forty nights.

The water grew higher and higher,
destroying all the wicked of the world.

Soon there was nothing and no one left alive in the world except for Noah, his family, and the animals on the ark.

When the rain finally stopped, Noah looked out at the earth and saw the flood rising higher and higher until mountains were covered with water.

The ark floated on the earth for 150 days. And on the seventh month and seventeenth day, it rested upon the mountain of Ararat.

But God did not forget Noah, for he sent a wind across the water until the flood began to go down. And soon the mountains could be seen again.

Noah set a dove free to to see if it was safe to open the ark.

But the dove could not find a place to rest
and returned to the ark.

Seven days later, Noah sent the dove out again. That evening she returned with an olive leaf in her mouth. Noah knew the flood had finally ended.

Noah waited another seven days and sent the dove out once more. This time she did not return.

Now Noah knew the water had dried; so he let out his wife and his sons, and all the birds and other animals from the ark.

Noah built a great altar to God and made offerings until God spoke to him once more.

God said, "While the earth remains, seedtime and harvest, summer and winter, and night and day shall not stop. . .

. . .Never again shall I send such a flood to destroy the earth."

And God sent a wonderful rainbow
as a sign of his promise to Noah.

To this day, man and all living things flourish on the earth.